COPENHAGEN

THE CITY AT A GLANCE

G000244107

Klampenborg

Optimistically referred to as the 'Danish Riviera', this stretch of land is known for its beaches, Arne Jacobsen architecture and its exclusivity. Be sure to have lunch at the Jacobsen restaurant.
See p097

Østerbro

One of Copenhagen's most affluent residential districts is well worth a visit for a spot of upmarket shopping.

Sankt Petri Church

The oldest surviving church in central Copenhagen, Sankt Petri dates to the 15th century. It was handed over to the city's German-speaking community by King Frederik II in 1585. Architect Hans Munk Hansen led its restoration in 1994.
Larslejsstræde 11, T 3393 3873

Town Hall

At 105m high, this 1905 building, known by locals as the *Rådhus*, dominates the low-rise Copenhagen skyline.
Rådhuspladsen 1

National Museum

Originally built in 1744 by Nicolai Eigtved, to house the Danish Royal Family, this museum now dedicates its 10,000 sq m of space to exhibits about Denmark's cultural history.
Ny Vestergade 10, T 3313 4411

INTRODUCTION
THE CHANGING FACE OF THE URBAN SCENE

Your arrival at Kastrup airport (see p067) will tell you a lot about Copenhagen: it's impeccably designed and impossibly efficient, yet maintains an unflustered air. The standard of living is said to be higher here than in any other capital city, yet life expectancy is, perversely, among the lowest in Europe. The reason for this is that the Danes know how to live, in all senses of the word. Not only do they design handsome buildings, but they eat, drink and inhale with great enthusiasm. That said, they don't seem to be affected by their hardly healthy lifestyle – they're an incredibly good-looking lot.

Of all the Scandinavian capitals, Copenhagen is the closest to mainland Europe and arguably the most cosmopolitan. Despite its sensible size, the city has a rich mix of things to do, see and take home. There is no better place to tackle by bike, as the city is both fantastically flat and architecturally rewarding. The legend of Arne Jacobsen looms large, although a new generation of Danish architects and designers has at last begun to emerge from his considerable shadow. Exploring furniture and interiors stores should prove a highlight of any trip, while shoppers more interested in fashion will have plenty to entice them too. Cultural distractions are not only numerous, but will inevitably be found in a building that you will be able to admire should the main event prove a disappointment. And, if even the building fails to enthral, there will always be a charming café just around the corner.

ESSENTIAL INFO

FACTS, FIGURES AND USEFUL ADDRESSES

TOURIST OFFICE
Vesterbrogade 4a
T 7022 2442
www.visitcopenhagen.com

TRANSPORT
Bicycle
www.bycyklen.dk
Car hire
Avis, *T 3251 2299*
Hertz, *T 3250 9300*
Metro
T 7015 1615
Taxis
Codan Taxi, *T 7025 2525*
Taxa 4x35, *T 3535 3535*

EMERGENCY SERVICES
Emergency
T 112
Police (non-emergencies)
Halmtovet 20 (4/b5)
T 3325 1448
24-hour pharmacy
Steno Apotek
Vesterbrogade 6c
T 3314 8266

CONSULATES
British Consulate
Kastelsvej 40
T 3544 5200
www.britishembassy.dk
US Consulate
Dag Hammerskjölds Alle 24
T 3341 7100
www.usembassy.dk
MONEY
American Express
Nørresgade 7a
T 3369 1101
www10.americanexpress.com

POSTAL SERVICES
Post Office
Tietgensgade 37
T 8020 7030
Shipping
UPS
T 3344 5580
www.ups.com

BOOKS
Arne Jacobsen: Works and Projects by Sola Guren De Corral and Felix Solaguren-Beascoa, translated by Graham Thomson (Gustavo Gili)
Room 606: The SAS House and the Work of Arne Jacobsen by Michael Sheridan (Phaidon Press)
Danish Chairs by Noritsugu Oda (Chronicle Books)

WEBSITES
Architecture/Design
www.arne-jacobsen.com
www.ddc.dk
Art
www.arken.dk
Newspapers
www.cphpost.dkr
www.jp.dk

COST OF LIVING
Taxi from Kastrup Airport to city centre
€23.50
Cappuccino
€3.60
Packet of cigarettes
€4.40
Daily newspaper
€1.40
Bottle of champagne
€66

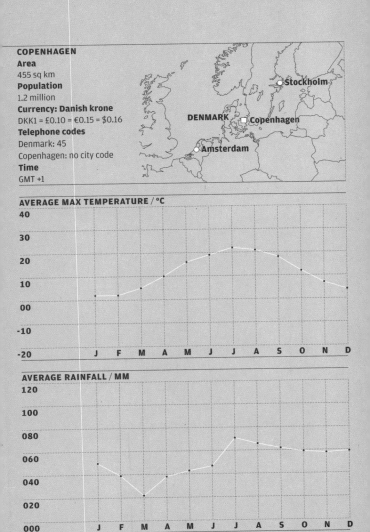

COPENHAGEN

Area
455 sq km
Population
1.2 million
Currency: Danish krone
DKK1 = £0.10 = €0.15 = $0.16
Telephone codes
Denmark: 45
Copenhagen: no city code
Time
GMT +1

Stockholm

DENMARK   Copenhagen

Amsterdam

AVERAGE MAX TEMPERATURE / °C

40
30
20
10
00
-10
-20

J F M A M J J A S O N D

AVERAGE RAINFALL / MM

120
100
080
060
040
020
000

J F M A M J J A S O N D

NEIGHBOURHOODS

THE AREAS YOU NEED TO KNOW AND WHY

To help you navigate the city, we've chosen the most interesting districts (see the map inside the back cover) and underlined featured venues in colour, according to their location (see below); those venues that are outside these areas are not coloured.

CITY

This is the established and elegant heart of Copenhagen, and is where visitors will spend the vast majority of their time. Streets such as Amagertorv make this a predominantly commercial area, but it also features many areas of historical interest, such as the Tivoli Gardens or Slotsholmen island. The area is sometimes also referred to as Indre By or Strøget, the name of the bustling pedestrianised street that runs through it.

CHRISTIANSHAVN

The artificial island of Christianshavn was created in the 17th century to protect the city against attack. The charming cobbled streets and old Dutch-style buildings are still very much in evidence, though today the area is a vibrant and trendy melting pot that attracts a mix of artists, businessmen and families; all are drawn by the picturesque setting, the world-class restaurants and the hip bars and cafés springing up in previously hidden corners.

VESTERBRO

With its old tenement buildings, the odd shady-looking character and a smattering of sex shops, Vesterbro is about as rough and ready as Copenhagen gets. A period of regeneration has been a civilising influence and the city's trendsetters are colonising the area with new shops and bars. It is also one of Copenhagen's nightlife hot spots.

NØRREBRO

Slightly shabbier than the pristine City area, multicultural Nørrebro has a more laid-back air, despite its proximity to the city centre. Home to numerous cafés and vintage fashion and furniture shops, it's become a popular place for young locals to spend their Saturdays.

ISLANDS BRYGGE

Although many of the city's cutting-edge companies, including numerous art galleries, have their HQs in Islands Brygge, it has yet to develop a year-round scene to support them. Come summer, however, the waterside strip that runs along one edge is packed with people until late at night, many of whom will be there to use the area's lovely outdoor pool (see p090).

FREDERIKSBERG

This upmarket area of tree-lined streets is actually an independent municipality within the city of Copenhagen. Until recently, it was a rather anonymous and sedate kind of place, but has become a little more lively thanks to a number of new restaurants, delis and boutiques.

ØSTERBRO

The preferred location for prosperous young families setting up home, Østerbro's many boutiques and facilities offer them all they need. Delicatessens, interiors stores and shops selling yoga mats can all be found along its wide streets.

LANDMARKS

THE SHAPE OF THE CITY SKYLINE

Unlike many of Europe's capitals, Copenhagen has few obvious landmarks. It's a city without many hills or tall buildings, making it hard to see much more than what is right in front of you. This, however, is no bad thing, as it enables you to appreciate the city up close. Orientation can be tricky, especially as the Metro network is limited and the stations are rarely immediately obvious to the eye. Water is perhaps the easiest way to get one's bearings; channels dotted with buildings, such as the Royal Library's 'Black Diamond' (see p062) and the Copenhagen Opera House (see p010), separate the City area from Christianshavn and Islands Brygge, while the 'Lakes' lie between the centre and the north-western districts.

If you are travelling around the centre by car or bike, you will often find yourself on two main roads, Hans Christian Andersens Boulevard, which cuts through the city along the west side, and Gothersgade, which does the same to the east. In between, the streets are smaller and more maze-like. A sprinkling of churches across Copenhagen can help with navigation, but the scale of the place is such that, at least in the City area, you are never far from your intended target. Residential neighbourhoods usually centre around a main shopping street: in Frederiksberg, this is Gammel Kongevej; in Østerbro, Østerbrogarde; in Nørrebro, Nørrebrogade and in Vesterbro, Vesterbrogade.

For all addresses, see Resources.

Copenhagen Opera House
Though some have been disappointed
by Henning Larsen's new building, it has
certainly become a notable spot on the
Copenhagen map, and dominates the
view along the water on the eastern side
of the city. It can also be admired from
the opposite bank, where a new Conran
development is leading the regeneration.
*Ekvipagemestervej 10, T 3369 6933,
www.operahus.dk*

Radisson SAS Royal Hotel

Completed in 1960, this building designed by Arne Jacobsen was the city's first major skyscraper, and is still one of its tallest structures. A shimmering rectangular box that reflects the sky (it appears grey in winter and blue in summer), the building is considered one of Jacobsen's greatest achievements. The Radisson SAS Royal marks the western edge of central Copenhagen and the start of Vesterbro. It is also located opposite the Central Station and famous fairground rides of Tivoli Gardens.
Hammerichgade 1, T 3815 6500
www.royalcopenhagen.radissonsas.com

Illums Bolighus

This legendary homewares store, which is set over four floors, marks the heart of the City district. Situated alongside the Royal Copenhagen, Holmegaard and Georg Jensen outlets on the main street of Amagertorv, Illums Bolighus is something of a shrine to Scandinavian design. Amagertorv's decorative paving, generous width and low-level buildings makes this pedestrian-only strip one of Europe's most attractive streets. More exclusive shopping areas can be found to the north-east of the city.

Amagertorv 10, T 3314 1941,
www.royalshopping.com

Dronning Louises Bro
This bridge, which was built in 1887 and designed by architect Vilhelm Dahlerup, is hardly Copenhagen's most remarkable structure, but it does allow great views across the 'Lakes', particularly at night. It is the middle of three bridges that cross the arc-shaped expanse of water that runs between the city centre and the districts of Østerbro, Nørrebro and Frederiksberg.

HOTELS

WHERE TO STAY AND WHICH ROOMS TO BOOK

Until relatively recently, the choice of hotels in Copenhagen was limited, to say the least. Room 606 at the Radisson SAS Royal Hotel (see p029) is still preserved almost exactly as Arne Jacobsen designed it more than 40 years ago. It seemed that this was the only bright spot in a barren landscape, and even this room had the melancholic air of a relic from the long-lost era when Denmark was at the forefront of international design. Today, things are changing, and there is a lot more choice in accommodation. Most attention-grabbing of all is the fabulously over-the-top Hotel Fox (opposite). Originally built in 2005 by Volkswagen, it was an extravagant and, some would say, desperate attempt to reflect some of the glory of the hotel onto their rather mundane 'Fox' car. Appearing like some sort of collision between an art college and a grand old hotel, the Fox is not for the faint-hearted.

Elsewhere in the city, the Copenhagen Hotel 27 (Løngangstræde 27, T 7027 5627) is undergoing a transformation into a respectable, if hardly ground-breaking, design-led hotel. And the recently opened Front (see p026) is heading in the same direction. Even Copenhagen's main youth hostel, the Danhostel (HC Andersens Boulevard 50, T 3311 8585), has recently enlisted the help of Danish design company Gubi (Klubiensvej 7-9, T 3332 6368) to add a bit of colour and sophistication to its interior.

For all addresses and room rates, see Resources.

Hotel Fox

As much exhibition spaces as places to spend the night (right down to the explanatory text panels beside each door), all of Hotel Fox's 61 rooms were handed over to graphic designers, illustrators and graffiti artists to design. As might be expected, the results range from the sublime to the ridiculous. While each of them will provide its occupants with a memorable stay, that's not always a good thing. We like the nature-themed Play Room (above), which was designed by the Akim Zasd Bus arts group. The hotel's in-house restaurant and bar both look good and serve fine food and drink, so if you can't quite face staying at the Fox, it's worth paying a visit for a cocktail or two or dinner.

Jarmers Plads 3, T 3313 3000,
www.hotelfox.dk

Lobby, Hotel Fox

Imperial Hotel

The exterior of this large hotel, situated just west of the city centre, near the Tivoli Gardens and the Town Hall, boasts some striking signage. The interior is not quite so stylish, however, and was designed mainly to suit the tastes of business travellers (all 214 rooms have satellite television and high-speed internet access). The entire hotel was renovated in 2006; we recommend opting for a standard double (opposite) or one of the more interesting rooms on the sixth floor, which all feature furniture by Danish designer Børge Mogensen. The Imperial's Garden Restaurant has its own butcher, baker and confectioner, and the hotel's glass-covered atrium is a pleasant place to sample their creations. The in-house brasserie is a popular spot with locals for Sunday brunch.
Vester Farimagsgade 9, T 3312 8000
www.imperialhotel.dk

Hotel Skt Petri

This hotel is housed in a graceful 1920s
building, designed by Wilhelm Lauritzen,
which was originally intended to be a
department store. It has fabulous views
of one of the prettiest parts of town,
and is situated close to the pedestrianised
shopping area. The Petri's cavernous lobby
(above) gives access to 268 rooms, which,
although hardly sensational, are all bright
and modern. Boasting five stars, the hotel
prides itself on its attentive service and
comprehensive facilities. Ask for a room
with a balcony or a terrace.
Krystalgade 22, T 3345 9100,
www.sktpetri.dk

Hotel Alexandra

This 61-room Alexandra, located in the city centre, is a perfect demonstration of the Danish concept of *hygge*, which roughly translates as 'cosy'. The hotel has been open for more than a century now and is an establishment that runs like clockwork. Rooms 223, 338 and 448 are each dedicated to a different Danish designer. We recommend Room 450 (above), which features furniture by Hans J Wegner. Another good option is Room 338, boasting, as it does, the wonderful creations of Finn Juhl. *HC Andersens Boulevard 8, T 3374 4444, www.hotel-alexandra.dk*

Front

Although very much following the boutique hotel formula, the recently opened Front does so with considerable aplomb. The fittings and furnishings have been well selected and the atmosphere is low-key but luxurious. The hotel's fitness centre will appeal to those who like to keep trim while they travel, and the option of MP3 players and maps for joggers is a nice touch. Bookish guests will appreciate the opportunity to settle down with the works of Karen Blixen (she was born just north of Copenhagen) by the open fire in the library. The 131-room hotel is situated near the waterfront, so you may want to ask for a room with a harbour view. Among our preferred rooms is 521 (right), which is done out in dusky, muted tones. It's not a room with a view, but it's spacious and comfortable.

Sankt Annæ Plads 21, T 3313 3400, www.front.dk

Bertrams

This is one of three hotels owned by the Guldsmeden group (Denmark's 'smallest hotel chain,' says Bertrams' owner Sandra Plesner Weinert). Most of its 47 rooms overlook either the street or a quieter courtyard to the rear, and each features a four-poster bed (above). The hotel subscribes to the 'less is more' philosophy and has an intimate, unpretentious feel. Bertrams' sister hotels are the Carlton (T 3322 1500), located in the up-and-coming Vesterbro neighbourhood, and the Aarhus, in the town of Aarhus, which is a few hours' drive from Copenhagen. *Vesterbrogade 107, T 3325 0405, www.hotelguldsmeden.dk*

Radisson SAS Royal Hotel

There is no doubt about which room to reserve here (well in advance). Room 606, also known as the Museum Room, has an entire book dedicated to it and remains almost exactly as it was when Arne Jacobsen completed the hotel in 1960. The Radisson's other rooms are rather uninspiring and similar to those in most other corporate hotels. Those higher up in the building (one of the only noticeably tall structures in Copenhagen) do have good views over the city. If you can't book 606, opt for the Royal Club Room (overleaf). On your way up, take a moment or two to linger in Jacobsen's lobby (above).

Hammerichsgade 1, T 3342 6000
www.radissonsas.com

Royal Club Room, Radisson SAS Royal Hotel

24 HOURS

SEE THE BEST OF THE CITY IN JUST ONE DAY

In a city as compact as Copenhagen, you can cover quite a bit of ground in one day. This itinerary is based mainly around the pretty central district, with one taxi ride out to the more rugged area around the docks. The upmarket municipality of Frederiksberg, with its leafy streets and parks, makes for a refined start to the day, and the main street, Gammel Kongeve, offers a multitude of eating options, Meyers Deli (opposite) being one of the best. After breakfast, head to the docklands in the north-east of the city, to see another side of Copenhagen (geographically and visually). Here you'll find the Paustian furniture store (see p034), a good introduction to your tour of the best in Danish design. When you return to the city centre, make sure you visit the four-floor interiors mecca Illums Bolighus (see p013), as well as the recently opened Hay (see p037). Make your way along the backstreets that link these shops, and you'll come across several other interesting stores that are well worth checking out.

All that walking or cycling, if you've really embraced the Danish way of life (see p089), should leave you looking forward to a cocktail or two and some supper. We recommend drinks at the excellent K Bar (see p038), then a taste of some Nordic cuisine with an experimental edge at Noma (Strandgade 93, T 3296 3297), which is over the water in Christianshavn.

For all addresses, see Resources.

09.00 Meyers Deli

There is only ever one 'plate' available on the breakfast menu at the smart Meyers Deli, located on the western side of the city. This changes throughout the year, but usually includes a selection of breads, meats and cheeses; yogurts, fresh fruit, croissants and pastries are also on offer. Accompany this with a black coffee (be warned, the Danes like it strong), then expect to make friends with the locals, as most of the seating is comprised of long, communal benches. Meyers is a great place for a weekend brunch. *Gammel Kongevej 107, T 3325 4595, www.meyersmad.dk*

11.00 Paustian

When you leave Meyers, take a taxi to Nordhavn, the north docks. If you have a little time on your hands, ask to stop first at Gubi (T 3332 6368), a huge furniture showroom with a spectacular backdrop of ships and containers. Your next destination, Paustian, is a truly magnificent interiors store and exhibition space, designed by Danish architect Jørn Utzon, of Sydney Opera House fame, and full of design treats. When you've worked up an appetite shopping, go for lunch in the Paustian restaurant, where chef Bo Bech prides himself on exciting even the most jaded taste buds.
Kalkbrænderiløbskaj 2, T 3916 6565, www.paustian.dk

14.00 National Bank

After lunch, make your way to Arne Jacobsen's National Bank. This was the great designer's last major project and was left unfinished when he died in 1971. An imposing building (as a bank should be), it has a spectacular lobby of awesome height. After your visit, stroll along the water to Café Stelling (T 3332 9300), another Jacobsen building and a great place to while away a few hours. Winter or summer, this is the best place in town to order a cup of hot chocolate. *Havnegade 5, T 3363 6363, www.nationalbanken.dk*

16.00 Hay

Thankfully, Copenhagen has largely avoided chain-store invasion and has a healthy network of independent outlets. The north-east corner of the City area is a great place to shop. The famous Illums Bolighus (see p013) is here, as is Hay (above), a furniture store selling mainly Danish designs. The shop's decor is understated but stylish, the range of items on display a reflection of the vision of the owner, Rolf Hay. When you've had your fill of interiors, check out the nearby fashion boutiques Holly Golightly (see p082) and Lot #29 (T 3314 1429). *Pilestræde 29-31, T 9942 4400, www.hay.dk*

20.00 K Bar
Finish your tour at this intimate little
place, where the staff take real pride
in the drinks they serve. The owner,
Kirsten Holm, has an encyclopedic
knowledge of cocktails and is on hand
if you're undecided about your order.
The house martini (citrus vodka and
mint-infused triple sec) is delicious.
Ved Stranden 20, T 3391 9222,
www.k-bar.dk

URBAN LIFE
CAFÉS, RESTAURANTS, BARS AND NIGHTCLUBS

As most places in Copenhagen tend to stay open until the early hours of the morning, locals usually eat late, then go out late, meeting friends for drinks in their neighbourhood bar. However, being out to see and be seen has never been big with the Danes, as they generally prefer to keep things low-key; most restaurants and bars have low-level lighting (often candles), which encourages intimacy rather than looking over your shoulder. Nightclubs have never been particularly popular here either, but if clubbing is something you must do, check out Vega (Enghavevej 40, T 3325 7011). Although the hip set have long since left this place behind, it invariably has a decent musical line-up and is worth a visit for its mostly original 1950s interior.

There is an impressive range of places to eat out in Copenhagen and almost every taste is catered for. French food goes down well, and the Danes are slowly taking Asian cuisine to their hearts. There has also been a resurgence of interest in traditional Nordic dishes, which often incorporate fish or beef and different grains. The city's thriving café culture means there are few better places to be than ensconced in a snug little corner with a coffee or a hot chocolate and a good book or newspaper. The service that you'll receive will almost always be very good – friendly but efficient – although staff will expect a healthy tip.

For all addresses, see Resources.

Søren K

Housed in the 'Black Diamond' (see p062), Søren K is a good reason to venture inside this controversial building. In keeping with its home, the restaurant is modern, with a minimalist interior. The menu is described as 'French-International', but includes good vegetarian options; the fresh seafood is excellent. Dishes are, for the most part, beautifully presented. Try to reserve a window table, so you can enjoy the views overlooking the canal. If you're eating here at lunchtime, visit the Royal Library in the same building after your meal.

Søren Kierkegaards Plads 1, T 3347 4949, www.soerenk.dk

Langelinie Pavillonen

Situated in a wonderful Mies van der Rohe-esque glass pavilion, built in 1958 and perched on the edge of Copenhagen port, Langelinie Pavillonen is one of the city's most elegant restaurants. Poul Henningsen's lamps, Arne Jacobsen 'Ant' chairs, Børge Mogensen sofas and Else Alfelts mosaics also make it a paean to Danish design. More and more, however, Langelinie Pavillonen is used solely as a venue for private parties and official functions; it's particularly popular with the fashion and media sets. If you do get invited to an event, take some time to step out on the terrace and look out over the Øresund; some parties even include a boat trip out to the Little Mermaid. The food served at Langelinie is fine – think fillet of catfish *au gratin* or roast breast of cockerel filled with foie gras.
Langelinie Pavillonen, T 3312 1214, www.langelinie.dk

Café Victor

Dare we say it, but the Danish take on the classic French brasserie might even be better than the time-honoured original. Café Victor is a great example, combining a wonderfully French fussiness (there's a zinc bar polished to shiny perfection and an impressive selection of wine, beers and spirits) with quiet Danish charm. Located just off the main shopping strip, Victor offers refuge from the grime and bustle of the city centre. Sit at a table perfectly set with a crisp white tablecloth and feel instantly revived.
Ny Østergade 8, T 3313 3613, www.cafevictor.dk

Granola

Granola is tiny little place in a quiet courtyard off Gammel Kongevej. Eating in can be tricky here, because of the lack of space, but it's a good place to grab a takeaway coffee, tea or freshly squeezed juice. There's always a delicious selection of pastries on offer, making this a popular spot for breakfast. Arriving later in the day is a good excuse to sample Granola's ice cream. If you're having trouble finding the place, look for a swinging orange sign with black and gold signage, then peer down the adjacent alley until you glimpse a yellow building with a white-tiled front.
Værnedamsvej 4, T 3325 0080

Koriander

Koriander's interior, which has strong
overtones of Stanley Kubrick's *2001:
A Space Odyssey*, announces this as a
restaurant of some ambition. Opened in
2005, under the direction of young chef
Singh Gill, Koriander serves a rather
unusual combination of Indian and French
cuisine. Following the lead of culinary
pioneers such as Ferran Adrià and Heston
Blumenthal, Gill pays little attention to
accepted ideas, preferring to carve out
his own culinary path, with dishes such
as veal with garam marsala, strawberries
and foie gras. It's easy to equate the
gleaming white interior with that of a
laboratory, but the green and gold cutlery
and heavy drapery make it a little more
opulent than that. And Gill's adventurous
instincts make Koriander much more than
yet another experiment in fusion cooking.
*Store Kongensgade 34, T 3315 0315,
www.restaurantkoriander.dk*

The Paul

The latest tenants of Poul Henningsen's spacious glass-domed theatre have already added considerable lustre to the gastronomic wasteland that is the Tivoli Gardens. English chef Paul Cunningham, who trained with Marco Pierre White, has introduced the Danes to hitherto unknown delights such as lemon curd, and seems to have won over both the public and critics with innovative tasting menus combing elements of British, French and Danish cuisine. The Michelin star, which was awarded to The Paul in 2004, cemented the restaurant's reputation as one of the best fine-dining options in the city.

Vesterbrogade 3, T 3375 0775,
www.thepaul.dk

The Laundromat Cafe

No activity is deemed too mundane to get the Nordic style treatment. Here, you can grab a cup of coffee in retro surrounds while washing your smalls in what must be the world's hippest launderette. Oh, and it sells second-hand books. As befits the vintage-chic of the neighbourhood, Nørrebro, the interior of The Laundromat is all worn wood and brightly coloured 1970s plastic. The menu is unpretentious and includes a 'dirty' or 'clean' brunch, burgers, sandwiches and salads. Good music, trendy diners and the hum of washing machines whirring away in the background keeps this place buzzing.
Elmegade 15, T 3535 2672,
www.thelaundromatcafe.com

Restaurant Ida Davidsen

They don't do dinner here, only a buffet lunch, which can be stretched out until closing time at 4pm, especially if the drinks are flowing. Ida Davidsen is Denmark's great smørrebrød specialist, and you'll often see her piling these open sandwiches high behind the counter. Businessmen and government officials keep this place busy, and the waiters don't always take too well to tourists.

To be welcomed like a local, we suggest ordering the 'Victor Borge' – salmon, marinated lumpfish caviar, crayfish tails, Greenland shrimps, and lime and dill mayonnaise – and several rounds of schnapps.
Store Kongensgade 70, T 3391 3655, www.idadavidsen.dk

Umami

This multi-level venue has been a big hit since it opened in May 2005. Created by British conceptual design team Orbit, it marries a restaurant space with a sushi bar upstairs and a sleek bar downstairs. Copenhagen's fashion set love the lemongrass sake cocktails and Japanese-style food.
Store Kongensgade 59, T 3338 7500, www.restaurantumami.dk

INSIDER'S GUIDE
THOMAS BEK, RETAIL MANAGER

Thomas Bek manages the fashion boutique Lot #29 (Gothersgade 29, T 3314 1429). If he's heading out for a quick bite, he makes a beeline for Le Le (Vesterbrogade 56, T 3322 7135); for a bowl of Vietnamese *pho*. 'It's cheap,' he says, 'but very good quality.' For a more leisurely meal, he recommends making a reservation at Le Sommelier (Bredgade 63-65, T 3311 4515), a restaurant that serves 'simple, honest Danish-French food, and has one of the longest wine lists in town'.

When shopping, Bek stocks up on cashmere at Lot #29, of course, but also pops into the 'very contemporary' Mads Nørgaard (Amagertorv 15, T 3332 0128), to snap up its own-label pieces and Rogan jeans. If he has time, he'll check out the exhibition on show at Galerie Asbæk (Bredgade 20, T 3315 4004), particularly if it's the work of Cathrine Raben Davidsen. Every August, Bek makes sure he books a ticket to see some modern ballet at the Bellevue Theatre (Strandvejen 451, T 3963 6400) in Klampenborg (see p097), an Arne Jacobsen-designed building with 'a very maritime feel to the interior'. Throughout the rest of the year, he likes to catch films at the Empire cinema in Nørrebro (Guldbergsgade 29, T 3536 0036): 'definitely the best seats in town'.

To round off an evening, it's usually cocktails at either Boutique Lize (Enghave Plads 6, T 3331 1560) or K Bar (see p038). Both, says Bek, serve 'excellent drinks and have a great ambience'.

ARCHITOUR

A GUIDE TO COPENHAGEN'S ICONIC BUILDINGS

Copenhagen has a distinguished architectural pedigree. This is a city where the notion of design is ingrained into the culture and good architecture is the norm, rather than a novelty. If you like your architecture to be towering, spectacular and daring, you've come to the wrong place; but if you like it to be lyrical, clean-lined and refined in its use of materials, you will find there's a lot to enjoy here. Of the modern architects, Kay Fisker and Arne Jacobsen have arguably made the biggest impact.

The Dronningegard Housing Scheme (Dronningens Tvaergade 23-45, Fredriksstaden), started in 1943 but completed in the late 1950s, was the work of Fisker, along with CF Moller and Sven Eske Kristensen. It is an intriguing sprawl of buildings, modern in execution but almost neoclassical in style. Jacobsen's restaurant (see p097) and gas station (see p100) outside Klampenborg are well worth a visit, while more central examples of his restrained, rarefied work include the Radisson SAS Royal Hotel (see p012 and p028) and the National Bank (see p034). Henning Larsen has been making his mark on the city, most notably with the eye-catching Copenhagen Opera House (see p010), though other recent structures have received a better public reaction. Look out for Knud Munk's Tycho Brahe Planetarium (Gammel Kongevej 10, T 3312 1224), one of Copenhagen's most recognisable buildings.

For all addresses, see Resources.

Tivoli Concert Hall

Tivoli Gardens, located in the city centre, is a 19th-century amusement park and one of the city's biggest tourist attractions. This being Denmark, the park is not as gaudy as you might think and is, in fact, a fairly impressive and striking sight. The thing to look out for, however, is not the fairground, but the extension to the Concert Hall, recently completed by architects 3XN. A large glass drum, with decorative aluminium ribbons running across it, the structure adds a lightness of touch to Tivoli. 3XN, one of Denmark's largest architectural firms, seems to be going from strength to strength, and this project proves why.
Tivoli Gardens, Vesterbrogade 3,
T 3315 1001, www.tivoli.dk

Interior, Tivoli Concert Hall

Grundtvigs Church

With its ziggurat shape and windowless facade, the yellow-brick Grundtvigs Church is one of the most distinctive landmarks in Copenhagen, albeit one in a rather anonymous residential district. Designed in the 1920s by Peder Vilhelm Jensen-Klint, the building is supposed to be an enlarged version of a Danish country church. Jensen-Klint's son, Kaare, who helped his father with the design and completed the building after his death, went on to become one of the most influential furniture and lighting designers of the 20th century. To visit the church, drive north-west of central Copenhagen for about 15 minutes, where you'll find it in the neighbourhood of Bispebjerg. *På Bjerget 14b, T 3581 5442, www.grundtvigskirke.dk*

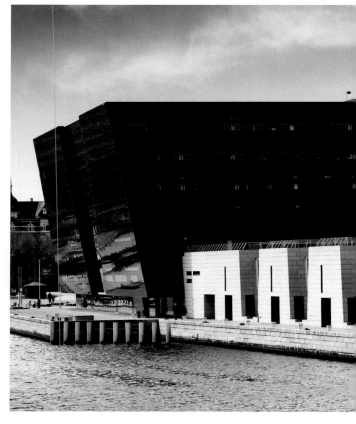

Black Diamond

This building, which juts out onto one of Denmark's canals, is an extension of the Royal Library. Called the Black Diamond, it is the work of Danish architects Bjarne Hammer, Morten Holm, Kim Holst Jensen, John E Lassen and Morten Schmidt. It opened in 1999, to massive attention, and that is only just starting to die down. Either a thing of sleek beauty or an aggressive shard of glass, or indeed both, depending on your viewpoint, there is no denying that it is a startling piece of architecture. For a while, the library had to ban curious visitors from ambling around the building because they were disturbing readers, but if you put on your most scholarly look and whisk in, you shouldn't be stopped. *Søren Kierkegaards Plads 1, T 3347 4747, www.kb.dk*

Arken Museum of Modern Art
Designed in the late 1980s by Søren
Robert Lund, Arken is a complex and
compelling building. Made largely from
steel, glass and concrete, the long,
horizontal aspect is in keeping with the
Danes' antipathy towards tall buildings.
Apparently, artists hate showing here,
because it is not in keeping with the
'white cube' image of an art gallery.
Skovvej 100, T 4354 0222, www.arken.dk

Bagsværd Church

Created by Jørn Utzon in 1974, this church looks almost industrial from the outside, yet inside it is as lyrical as modern architecture gets. An undulating ceiling and Utzon's masterly manipulation of space combine to sensational effect. With its white ceilings and walls, the church has been designed to absorb as much light as possible. 'It is the light that is the most important feature of this church,' Utzon has said. This is another architectural destination that you will have to drive to, but it's certainly worth the trip.
Taxvej 14, www.bagsvaerdkirke.dk

Kastrup Airport

We can only hope that, one day, all airports will be designed like this one. And, as it gets bigger, it only gets better. The 2001 extension by Holm & Grut has teak flooring that seems to take all the strain out of pushing your luggage cart, while the glass control tower, completed in 2005, has picked up a number of architectural awards. If you arrive at the airport at dusk, when the wooden structure that juts out into the sea is softly lit by up-lights, it is a gorgeous sight. Nearby, you'll find the Kastrup Sea Bath (Amager Strandvej 301), an outdoor pool designed by the Swedish architects White. *Lufthavnsboulevarden 6, T 3231 3231, www.cph.dk*

Øresund Link

One of Copenhagen's largest structures,
this 7,845m bridge, opened in 2000
and designed by Dissing + Weitling and
Georg Rotne, joins the Danish capital
to southern Sweden. It is much admired
for its geometric rhythm and stark
appearance, though some may prefer
the Storebælt Bridge, which connects
Copenhagen to Funan.
www.oresundskonsortiet.com

SHOPPING
THE CITY'S BEST SHOPS AND WHAT TO BUY

Until recently, the only thing to shop for in Copenhagen was home-wares. Lighting, clocks, tableware and crockery, and perhaps a few pieces of furniture, were the things to ship back home. But these days, it's worth making a little space in your luggage (or crate, depending on how serious a shopper you are) for a few items of clothing. While Danish furniture and product design is still dominated by the great names of the past, although this is changing, the Danish fashion scene feels remarkably fresh. The huge Normann store (see p086), in Østerbro, houses both strands of Danish design, but if it's just clothes you're after, head to the north-east edge of the city centre, off Gothersgade, where you'll find a number of tempting boutiques. The largest and most comprehensively stocked of these is Storm (Store Regnegade 1, T 3393 0014), but you'll also come across others with a little more character.

When it comes to interiors, it's tempting to feel satisfied by Illums Bolighus (see p013), but this would mean missing out on much else the city has to offer. Check out the vintage design stores on Bredgade in the centre, or the slightly more ramshackle shops on Ravnsborggade in Nørrebro. Other items to bring home include food (a number of decent new delis have opened recently), bikes (see p089) and anything by Bang & Olufsen (Kongens Nytorv 26, T 3311 1415), be it vintage or new.

For all addresses, see Resources.

Retrograd

Our favourite shop in Islands Brygge stocks everything from porcelain to tableware. Opened in 2003, this small basement store was created by Signe Jarf and Mogens Petersen. Selling vintage furnishings and household items from the 1950s and 60s, it's a treasure trove for any design collector. Educated at the Royal Danish Academy of Fine Arts, Jarf also has a studio at the back of the store, where she works on paintings that are then exhibited or sold in galleries. Expect to find an eclectic range of products on sale at Retrograd. We loved this teacup, DKK125, saucer, DKK75 and matching sugar pot, DKK35 (all above).
Gunløgsgade 7, T 2241 4657

Modern 10a

The Nørrebro district is littered with interesting little antique and bric-a-brac shops. Modern 10a is one of the best, and sells a range of modern Danish classics at surprisingly reasonable prices. This red aluminium 'Flower Pot' pendant light (above), DKK550, was designed by Verner Panton, a pioneer of the futuristic style of the 1960s. When you leave Modern 10a, continue your retro tour by calling in at the nearby 1970s-inspired Laundromat Cafe (see p049), for a coffee or a snack. *Ravnsborggade 10A*

Ole Madsen Antiktanken & Design

Ole Madsen takes immense pride in his shop, which sells a selection of mostly mid-20th century Scandinavian design, though Madsen will also offer up earlier pieces if they meet his exacting standards – all items on sale In Antiktanken & Design are in perfect condition. We snapped up these wooden candlesticks (above), by Danish designer Kay Bojesen, for DKK400. The shop is located on Ravnsborggade, just off Sankt Hans Torv, a hip street that's popular with locals and visitors alike for its clothing boutiques and antique stores. *Ravnsborggade 21, T 4020 2024*

My Bikes

If you don't consider yourself to be particularly taken with bicycles, My Bikes will make you think again; even ardent car drivers could be converted to pedal power after an hour or so in the store. While non-bikers will admire the pure forms and striking colours of Rasmus Gjesing's beautiful two-wheeled creations, the cycling set will fall in love with his immaculate craftsmanship. Gjesing has been in business as a bicyclemaker since 1995, and since then he has picked up numerous fans, including American design aficionado Murray Moss, who invited him to sell through his New York store, Moss (T 00 1 212 204 7100), and Paul Smith, who bought one for himself. Most of Gjesing's bikes are bespoke creations, though you'll also find 'off-the-peg' models in the showroom. *Store Kongensgade 57, T 3311 1211, www.mybikes.dk*

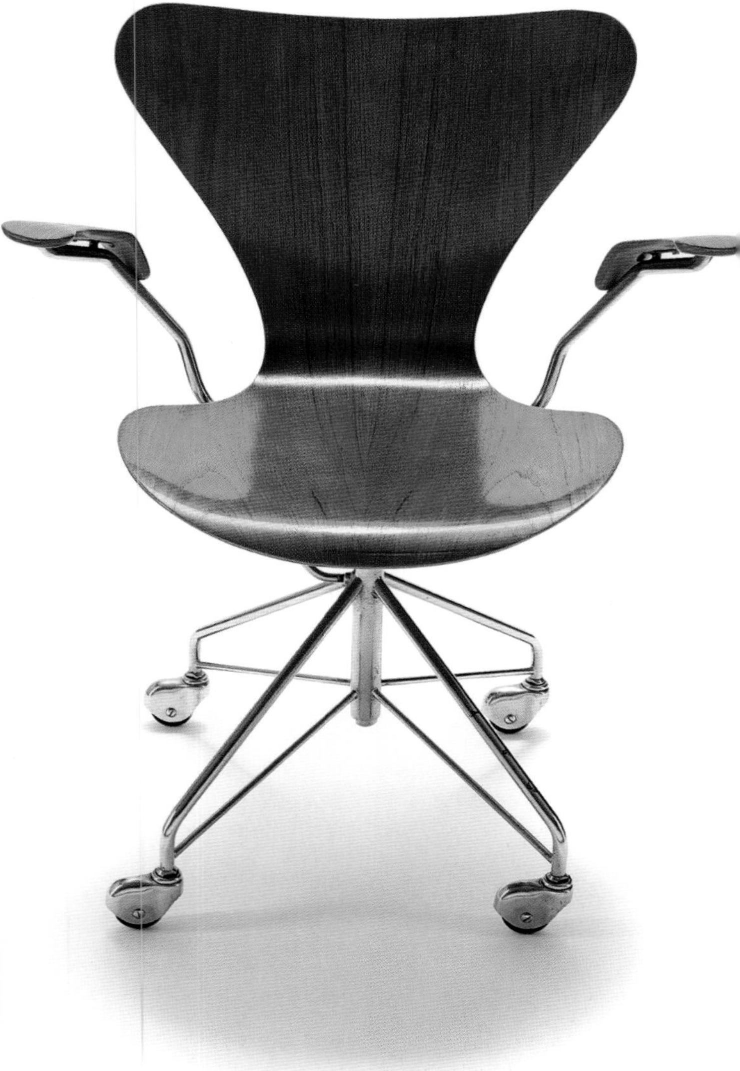

Kolmorgen

The owners of this company take great pride in being the largest exporters of vintage Danish furniture and interiors, to almost every part of the world. You can take a peak in their showroom, which has a selection of teak, rosewood, oak and steel furniture from the 1940s to the 1970s on display, but to see the wider collection or to make a purchase, you'll have to visit their website. Classics you may come across include this Arne Jacobsen chair (left), price on request, and wooden toys by Kay Bojesen, such as the car, DKK575, and train, DKK1350 (above). Kolmorgen also stocks pieces by Børge Mogensen and Hans J Wegner. *Bredgade 10, T 2170 8792, www.kolmorgen.com*

Holly Golightly

This tiny boutique can be spotted by its lemon-yellow awning. Inside, you'll find a carefully selected range of women's clothes, accessories, beauty products and a cute collection of childrenswear. Many of the items are designed by the likes of Marni, Edun, Balenciaga and Marc Jacobs, which can all be hard to find elsewhere in Denmark. Besides clothes, there are a number of items that the owners have picked up on their travels around the world; we liked the striped Italian toothbrushes. Holly Golightly's light interior, which is complemented by large, gold-framed mirrors, and immaculate packaging (everything is wrapped in heart-covered tissue paper) are sure to guarantee you make a return visit when you are next in town.

Gammel Mønt 2, T 3314 1915,
www.hollygolightly.dk

Georg Jensen

Danish silversmith Georg Jensen began trading from a tiny silver store in the heart of Copenhagen in 1904. Today, the company has branches all over the world, including a Beverly Hills shop on Rodeo Drive opened in June 2006, designed by Tadao Ando. While the Copenhagen store (left) may not be quite so cutting-edge, its three spacious floors show off Jensen's simple, timeless designs to great effect. Come here to pick up a Jensen classic or something a little more quirky, such as this men's 'Aracdaia' ring, DKK 1,100 (above).
Amagertorv 4, T 3311 4080,
www.georgjensen.com

Normann
Housed in an former cinema, this
is a boutique on a grand scale.
The cavernous interior showcases
Normann's clever little accessories,
which are stacked up in the entrance,
along with a range of furniture,
fashion and homewares from the
rest of Scandinavia and beyond.
Østerbrogade 70, T 3555 4459,
www.normann-copenhagen.com

SPORTS AND SPAS
WORK OUT, CHILL OUT OR JUST WATCH

If you cross Copenhagen at rush hour, you'll see that people in this city are not afraid to be active. The sheer number of bicycles pushing their way through the streets, even in the grimmest weather, is a sight to behold. While many Danes undoubtedly like cigarettes, drink and a less than healthy diet, they're also prepared to tough it out in the gym, in the pool or on the field. For this reason, sports facilities are not hard to find, and if you want to take a run (we recommend heading for Ørstedsparken, near Nørreport Station), you won't be jogging alone.

Perhaps the easiest place for visitors to exercise is the DGI-byen sports centre (Tietgensgade 65, T 3329 8000, www.dgi-byen.com), near Central Station. It offers a range of activities, including climbing, and has an extensive Swim Centre. Øbro-Hallen (Gunnar Nu Hansens Plads 3, T 3525 7060) is also a great place to take a dip. It might not be quite as state-of-the-art as DGI-byen, but the recently refurbished building lacks little in terms of visual splendour.

While the Danes aren't necessarily passionate about spectator sports, there is still a large following for football – FC Copenhagen is the city's biggest club – and, to a lesser extent, handball and ice hockey. At FC's stadium, Parken (Øster Alle 50, T 3543 3131, www.parken.dk), in Østerbro, you'll not only find a football ground, but also an indoor ice rink.

For all addresses, see Resources.

Sögreni

If you really want to get into the spirit of the city, you should explore it on two wheels. The 'Louisiana' bicycle (above) was designed by legendary local bike manufacturer Sögreni, as a gift for the founder of Copenhagen's Louisiana Museum of Modern Art (T 4919 0791). With its simple steel frame and classic Brooks saddle, it certainly makes for a stylish ride. Each Sögreni bicycle is lovingly crafted by hand and costs around DKK9,500. If you're tempted to buy one, visit the store or the shop at the Louisiana. Ride out from the museum along the North Zealand coast, looking out as you go across the sound to Sweden.
Sankt Pedersstræde 30a, T 3312 7879, www.sogreni.dk

Copenhagen Harbour Bath
Designed by Plot, a celebrated but
now defunct architectural firm, and
completed in 2003, the Copenhagen
Harbour Bath has proved a resounding
success. Its five pools use water from
the ultra-clean Islands Brygge channel.
The terraced seating area gets packed
out in summer and is open from 7am
during the week.
Havnefronten Islands Brygge, T 2371 3189

Østerbro Stadion

Østerbro Stadion is the home of the obscurely named B.93 football team. Overshadowed by the far larger but blander Parken stadium (T 3543 3131), home of FC Copenhagen, Østerbro may be small, but it certainly has character. Bronze statues of naked athletes display themselves at various points around the ground and the clubhouse is a building of austere beauty. You can come to watch the B.93 team play and also use the athletics track that surrounds the pitch, if you ask permission in advance.
Gunnar Nu Hansens Plads 7, T 3526 4536

Rosenborg Spa
Housed in a renovated 19th-century
building, this spa offers classic
treatments in a sumptuous setting.
Twinkling chandeliers and flickering
candles add an air of grandeur and make
guests feel far away from the streets
below. Come here to sip champagne
in your own private bathing room.
*Kronprinsessegade 20, T 3332 3005,
www.rosenborgspa.dk*

ESCAPES

WHERE TO GO IF YOU WANT TO LEAVE TOWN

Thanks to reliable road and rail networks, taking trips from Copenhagen shouldn't prove problematic, and there are plenty of destinations to head for. During the summer, you'll find many locals making their way to a nearby beach. Although it's unlikely that you've travelled to Denmark to seek out the sun, there are still a few good places to take your towel and factor 20. Try the beaches of Bellevue Strand, on what's known, with no apparent irony, as the 'Danish Riviera', or Amager Strand, which was extensively landscaped in 2005. Another beach, Ishøj Strand, has the added attraction of the Arken Museum of Modern Art (see p064), a stunning concrete, steel and glass building by Søren Robert Lund. Klampenborg (opposite) not only has an appealing beach, but it's the best place to enjoy the architecture of Arne Jacobsen.

Another escape option is to head for Malmö (see p102), the Swedish city located approximately an hour away via the Øresund Link bridge (see p070). The fact that far more Swedes travel to Copenhagen than Danes journey to Malmö might sound off-putting, but the spectacular bridge crossing alone will make it worth your while. The Louisiana Museum of Modern Art (Gammel Strandvej 13, Humlebæk, T 4919 0791) is recommended not just for its collection of 20th-century art, but because it's the kind of quiet, assured place that one would find only in Scandinavia. *For all addresses, see Resources.*

Klampenborg

Arne Jacobsen's presence can be felt strongly across Copenhagen: from the 'Series 7' and 'Egg' chairs frequently seen in cafés, hotel lobbies and antique stores to the numerous buildings he designed across the capital. It's easy to see why Jacobsen's influence is so widespread, as the great Dane was clearly an immensely inspired designer, architect, gardener and artist. Perhaps the best way to take in his talents is to head north to the wealthy residential district of Klampenborg, which can be reached via a short but satisfying drive along the Øresund coastal road. On arrival, you can nose around the Bellavista housing estate, have lunch at the Jacobsen restaurant (T 3963 4322; overleaf) and even fill up at the Jacobsen-designed petrol station (see p100).

Arne Jacobsen Petrol Station
On the Øresund coastal road, stop at
this petrol station in Charlottenlund,
near Klampenborg. Perhaps the most
architecturally significant place to refill
your gas-guzzler, it's a small building
and forecourt designed for Texaco by
Arne Jacobsen in 1937. It's still in use
and lovingly maintained (which makes
a change), although it's now self-service.
Skovshoved Harbour, Charlottenlund

HSB Turning Torso

This gravity-defying residential tower in Malmö, Sweden, is just 20 minutes from Copenhagen. Designed by Santiago Calatrava, the 190m Turning Torso began life as an abstracted sculpture of the human body in motion. That sculpture is now 54 floors of concrete comprising of nine 'box units'. Each unit is composed of five floors of apartments, with all services located close to the concrete core, freeing up the outer facade for unrestricted views of the dramatic Øresund landscape. The interiors have been designed by Samark Arkitektur & Design AB, with attention paid to the smallest of things, such as mixer taps by Philippe Stark. Besides the view, the tower pampers its guests with a gym, sauna and even a private wine cellar. The first 10 floors are given over to office space, the 49th to the Panorama Room.

Lilla Varvsgatan 14, Malmö, Sweden,
T 00 46 4035 7739, www.turningtorso.com

Dear Reader, Books by Phaidon are recognised world-wide for their beauty, scholarship and elegance. We invite you to return this card with your name and e-mail address so that we can keep you informed of our new publications, special offers and events. Alternatively, visit us at **www.phaidon.com** to see our entire list of books, videos and stationery. Register on-line to be included on our regular e-newsletters.

Subjects in which I have a special interest

☐ General Non-Fiction   ☐ Art   ☐ Photography   ☐ Architecture   ☐ Design

☐ Fashion   ☐ Music   ☐ Children's   ☐ Food   ☐ Travel

Mr/Miss/Ms   Initial   Surname

Name

No./Street

City

Post code/Zip code   Country

E-mail

This is not an order form. To order please contact Customer Services at the appropriate address overleaf.

Please delete address *not* required before mailing

PHAIDON PRESS INC.

180 Varick Street

New York

NY 10014

PHAIDON PRESS LIMITED

Regent's Wharf

All Saints Street

London N1 9PA

*Affix
stamp
here*

NOTES

SKETCHES AND MEMOS

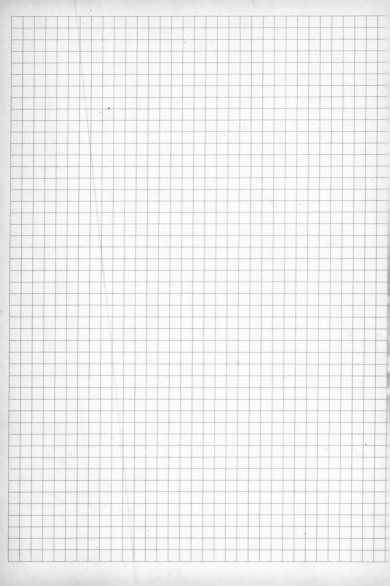

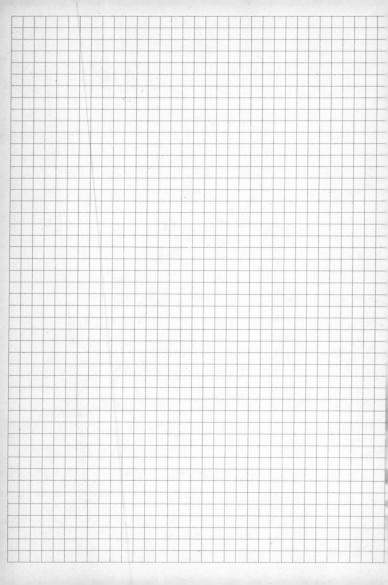

RESOURCES
ADDRESSES AND ROOM RATES

LANDMARKS

010 Copenhagen Opera House
Ekvipagemestirvej 10
T 3369 6933
www.operahus.dk

011 Radisson SAS Royal Hotel
Hammerichgade 1
T 3815 6500
www.royalcopenhagen.
radissonsas.com

013 Illums Bolighus
Amagertorv 10
T 3314 1941
www.royalshopping.com

HOTELS

016 Copenhagen Hotel 27
Room rates:
double, DKK1,390
Løngangstræde 27
T 7027 5627
www.hotel27.dk

016 Danhostel
Room rates:
double, DKK520
HC Andersens Boulevard 50
T 3311 8585
www.danhostel.dk

017 Hotel Fox
Room rates:
double, DKK1,120;
Play Room, DKK1,120
Jarmers Plads 3
T 3313 3000
www.hotelfox.dk

020 Imperial Hotel
Room rates,
double, DKK1,700
Vester Farmagsgade 9
T 3312 8000
www.imperialhotel.dk

022 Hotel Skt Petri
Room rates,
double, DKK1,995
Krystalgade 22
T 3345 9100
www.sktpetri.dk

023 Hotel Alexandra
Room rates:
double, DKK1,365;
Rooms 223, 338 448
and 450, DKK1,965
HC Andersens Boulevard 8
T 3374 4444
www.hotel-alexandra.dk

026 Front
Room rates:
double, DKK1,590;
Room 521, DKK2,790
Sankte Annæ Plads 21
T 3313 3400
www.front.dk

028 Bertrams
Room rates:
double, DKK1,495
Vesterbrogade 107
T 3325 0405
www.hotelguldsmeden.dk

028 Aarhus
Room rates:
double, DKK1,095
Guldsmedgade 40
Aarhus
T 8613 4550
www.hotelguldsmeden.dk

028 Carlton
Room rates:
double, DKK1,375
Vesterbrogade 66
T 3322 1500
www.hotelguldsmeden.dk

029 Radisson SAS Royal Hotel
Room rates:
double, DKK1,995;
Room 606, DKK4,900;
Royal Club Room,
DKK2,595
Hammerichsgade 1
T 3342 6000
www.radissonsas.com

24 HOURS

032 Noma
Strandgade 93
T 3296 3297
www.noma.dk

033 Meyers Deli
Gammel Kongevej 107
T 3325 4595
www.meyersmad.dk

034 Paustian
Kalkbrænderiløbskaj 2
T 3916 6565
www.paustian.dk

034 Gubi
Klubiensvej 7-9
T 3332 6368
www.gubi.dk

036 National Bank
Havnegade 5
T 3363 6363
www.nationalbanken.dk

036 Café Stelling
Gammeltorv 6
T 3332 9300
037 Hay
Pilestræde 29-31
T 9942 4400
www.hay.dk
037 Lot#29
Gothersgade 29
T 3314 1429
www.lot29.dk
038 K Bar
Ved Stranden 20
T 3391 9222
www.k-bar.dk

URBAN LIFE
040 Vega
Enghavevej 40
T 3325 7011
www.vega.dk
041 Søren K
Søren Kierkegaards
Plads 1
T 3347 4949
www.soerenk.dk
041 Langelinie
Pavillonen
Langelinie Pavillonen
T 3312 1214
www.langelinie.dk
044 Café Victor
Ny Østergade 8
T 3313 3613
www.cafevictor.dk
045 Granola
Værnedamsvej 4
T 3325 0080

046 Koriander
Store Kongensgade 34
T 3315 0315
www.restaurant
koriander.dk
048 The Paul
Vesterbrogade 3
T 3375 0775
www.thepaul.dk
049 The Laundromat Cafe
Elmegade 15
T 3535 2672
www.thelaundromat
cafe.com
050 Restaurant
Ida Davidsen
Store Kongensgade 70
T 3391 3655
www.idadavidsen.dk
052 Umami
Store Kongensgade 59
T 3338 7500
www.restaurantumami.dk
054 Bellevue Theatre
Strandvejen 451
T 3963 6400
054 Boutique Lize
Enghave Plads 6
T 3331 1560
054 Empire
Guldbergsgade 29
T 3536 0036
054 Galerie Asbæk
Bredgade 20
T 3315 4004

054 Le Le
Vesterbrogade 56
T 3322 7135
054 Le Sommelier
Bredgade 63-65
T 3311 4515
www.lesommelier.dk
054 Mads Nørgaard
Amagertorv 15
T 3332 0128
www.madsnorgaard.dk

ARCHITOUR
056 Dronningegard
Housing Scheme
Dronningens Tvaergade
23-45
Fredriksstaden
056 Tycho Brahe
Planetarium
Gammel Kongevej 10
T 3312 1224
www.tycho.dk
057 Tivoli Concert Hall
Tivoli Gardens
Vesterbrogade 3
T 3315 1001
www.tivoli.dk
060 Grundtvigs Church
På Bjerget 14b
T 3581 5442
www.grundtvigskirke.dk
062 Black Diamond
Royal Library
Søren Kierkegaards Plads 1
T 3347 4747
www.kb.dk

064 Arken Museum of Modern Art
Skovvej 100
T 4354 0222
www.arken.dk

066 Bagsværd Church
Taxvej 14
www.bagsvaerdkirke.dk

067 Kastrup Airport
Lufthavnsboulevarden 6
T 3231 3231
www.cph.dk

056 Kastrup Sea Bath
Amager Strandvej 301

070 The Øresund Link
www.oresunds konsortiet.com

070 Storebælt Bridge
www.storebaelt.dk

SHOPPING

072 Storm
Store Regnegade 1
T 3393 0014

072 Bang & Olufsen
Kongens Nytorv 26
T 3311 1415
www.bang-olufsen.com

073 Retrograd
Gunløgsgade 7
T 2241 4657

076 Modern 10a
Ravnsborggade 10a

077 Ole Madson Antiktanken & Design
Ravnsborggade 21
T 4020 2024

078 My Bikes
Store Kongensgade 57
T 3311 1211
www.mybikes.dk

078 Moss
146 Greene Street
New York, USA
T 00 1 212 204 7100
www.mossonline.com

080 Kolmorgen
Bredgade 10
T 2170 8792
www.kolmorgen.com

082 Holly Golightly
Gammel Mønt 2
T 3314 1915
www.hollygolightly.dk

084 Georg Jensen
Amagertorv 4
T 3311 4080
www.georgjensen.com

086 Normann
Østerbrogade 70
T 3555 4459
www.normann-copenhagen.com

SPORTS AND SPAS

088 DGI-byen
Tietgensgade 65
T 3329 8000
www.dgi-byen.com

088 Øbro-Hallen
Gunnar Nu Hansens Plads 3
T 3525 7060

088 Ørstedsparken
Near Nørreport Station

089 Sögreni
Sankt Pedersstræde 30a
T 3312 7879
www.sogreni.dk

089 Louisiana Museum of Modern Art
Gammel Strandvej 13
Humlebæk
T 4919 0791
www.louisiana.dk

090 Copenhagen Harbour Bath
Havenfronten
Islands Brygge
T 2371 3189

092 Østerbro Stadion
Gunnar Nu Hansens Plads 7
T 3526 4536
www.b93.dk

092 Parken
Øster Alle 50
T 3542 3131
www.parken.dk

094 Rosenborg Spa
Kronprinsessegade 20
T 3332 3005
www.rosenburgspa.dk

ESCAPES

097 Jacobsen
Strandvejen 449
Klampenborg
T 3963 4322
www.restaurant jacobsen.dk

100 Arne Jacobsen Petrol Station
Skorshoved Harbour
Charlottenlund

102 HSB Turning Torso
Lilla Varvsgatan 14
Malmö, Sweden
T 00 46 4035 7739
www.turningtorso.com

WALLPAPER* CITY GUIDES

Editorial Director
Richard Cook

Art Director
Loran Stosskopf
City Editor
Albert Hill
Project Editor
Rachael Moloney
Series Editor
Jeroen Bergmans
Executive Managing Editor
Jessica Firmin

Chief Designer
Ben Blossom
Designers
Sara Martin
Ingvild Sandal
Map Illustrator
Russell Bell

Photography Editor
Christopher Lands
Photography Assistant
Jasmine Labeau

Sub-Editors
Emily Mathieson
Paul Sentobe

Editorial Assistants
Felicity Cloake
Milly Nolan

Wallpaper* Group Editor-in-Chief
Jeremy Langmead
Creative Director
Tony Chambers
Publishing Director
Fiona Dent

Thanks to
Paul Barnes
Thomas Bentzen
David McKendrick
Meirion Pritchard
James Reid

PHAIDON

Phaidon Press Limited
Regent's Wharf
All Saints Street
London N1 9PA

Phaidon Press Inc
180 Varick Street
New York, NY 10014

www.phaidon.com

First published 2006
© 2006 Phaidon
Press Limited

ISBN 0 7148 4685 6

A CIP Catalogue record
for this book is available
from the British Library.

All rights reserved.
No part of this publication
may be reproduced,
stored in a retrieval system
or transmitted, in any
form or by any means,
electronic, mechanical,
photocopying, recording
or otherwise, without
the prior permission of
Phaidon Press.

All prices are correct at
time of going to press,
but are subject to change.

Printed in China

PHOTOGRAPHERS

Thomas Ibsen
Copenhagen City View,
inside front cover
Copenhagen Opera
House, pp010-011
Radisson SAS Royal
Hotel, p012
Illums Bolighus, p013
Dronning Louises
Bro, pp014-015
Paustian, pp034-035
Jacobsen's National
Bank, p036
K Bar, pp038-039
Søren K, p041
Langelinie Pavillonen,
pp042-043
Café Victor, p044
Granola, p045
Koriander, pp046-047
The Paul, p048
The Laundromat Cafe, p049
Restaurant Ida Davidsen,
pp050-051
Umami, pp052-053
Thomas Bek, p055
Tivoli Concert Hall,
p057, pp058-059
Grundtvigs Church,
pp060-061
Black Diamond,
pp062-063
Arken Museum of
Modern Art, pp064-065
Bagsværd Church, p066
Kastrup Airport,
p067, pp068-069

Øresund Link, pp070-071
My Bikes, pp078-079
Arne Jacobsen chair,
Kay Bojesen toys,
pp080-081
Holly Golightly, pp082-083
Copenhagen Harbour
Bath, pp090-091
Ørstebro Stadion,
pp092-093
Rosenborg Spa,
pp094-095
Klampenborg, p097
Jacobsen restaurant,
pp098-099
Arne Jacobsen petrol
station, pp100-101

**Line Falck, Kam & Co
Denmark**
Meyers Deli, p033

Pierre Mens
HSB Turning Torso, p102

Jason Tozer
Teacup, saucer,
sugar pot, p073,
Retrograd, pp074-075
Verner Panton 'Flower Pot'
light, p076
Kay Bojesen
candlesticks, p077
'Louisiana' bicycle, p089

COPENHAGEN
A COLOUR-CODED GUIDE TO THE CITY'S HOT 'HOODS

CITY
The (mostly) elegant heart of the city, even if Tivoli is starting to fade a little

CHRISTIANSHAVN
All gables and cobbles, this charming island is a sublime spot for strolling

VESTERBRO
Even the city's red-light district is enviably good-looking. Definitely an area on the up

NØRREBRO
Traditionally, this is the place to seek out those vintage shopping bargains

ISLANDS BRYGGE
In summer, this waterside area comes into its own; avoid it in the winter, though

FREDERIKSBERG
Always an anomaly, this city-within-a-city is slowly shedding its staid, suburban image

ØSTERBRO
Yummy-mummy territory and so a little bit smug, but well stocked with fine delis

For a full description of each neighbourhood,
including the places you really must not miss, see the Introduction